Joy Comes with the Mourning

Christina Maldonado

BookLeaf
Publishing

Presentation by *BookLeaf Publishing*

Web: www.bookleafpub.com

E-mail: info@bookleafpub.com

ISBN: 9789357442060

First edition 2023

DEDICATION

In Memory of Kristina Rivera

Static Snow

This time last year
I was static on an old TV.
Fragments of hope and despair
in the harshest black and white.
Snowflakes and ink blots.
13 days between goodbye
and hello to a new year
without you in it.
Sleigh bells and teardrops.
Heart empty as
Bethlehem's manger,
waiting for Him to arrive.
Come, Emmanuel:
God with me.
Let my weary soul rejoice.

The Wasting

Tendons and joints
betraying bones.
Irregular cells
masquerading and
infiltrating.
We pity the obviously dying,
ignoring our own slow decay.
All of creation groans
in anticipation and longing
for a reality we traded
like Esau's birthright.
A bowl of stew and an apple
left us forever hungry.
There will be a day when
He will wipe away all tears,
and the banquet we have ached for
will be ours.

Returned to Sender

When I return to the dust,
I hope to become part of the soil
and root system of a mighty tree
that is eventually
harvested for stationery.

The expensive kind.

Perhaps an appreciator of old ways
will select that paper
specifically with the intention of
sending a letter.

One that requires a stamp.

Yes, I want to be a love letter.
For now I will try to live as one
until I am returned to my Sender.

Harvest

If we are to reap joy
from the tears that we've sown,
I am expecting nothing less.
If every drop is a seed,
there should be rippling fields
of vibrant wildflowers dancing
and rainforests of giggling brooks
waiting for me.

For now I am wandering in the desert,
unable to receive the Promised Land.
For now I am learning to trust Him
for my daily bread.
Like a lamb with an injured leg,
I lash out at my Shepherd.
The One who feeds me.
Sustains me.
Protects me.

Someday He and I will run
through those fields,
and He will lead me to the water.

Thirty-Three

Your soft, pained moans
will stay with me for
the rest of my life.
What did you want to say?
The raspy gurgling of lungs
that had grown too tired
betrayed you.
You were only 33.

When you entered His Kingdom
and took the first satisfying breath
you had ever known,
I imagine He took you in His arms
and whispered,
"So was I."

He, too, was bruised and broken.
He, too, experienced unimaginable agony.
He, too, felt the bitter sting of loneliness.
He, too, left His mother in the care of others.

Every prayer you wondered
if He'd even heard
was captured and brought before Him

as the sweetest incense.
Every tear you thought you'd
cried in vain was collected and sealed
in His lachrymatory bottles.

Now, in the halls of heaven,
you join the chorus of angels
with worship purer than
refined gold.
The King will return!
He will reign forever!
You shout with a strength
unknown to us here:
"SO WILL I!"

Arms

There is a longing
to be held in arms
that seek nothing in return.
To be satisfied with my purpose
and fit into some grand plan
like the gears of a clock:
Dependent but useful.
The only arms holding me now
are the ones slowly ticking
further away from each other.
I slide off the minute hand,
landing face to clock face.
The reverberating tocks
drum unevenly with my racing heart.

If a day is as a thousand years to You,
I'm only asking for a few moments
enveloped in everlasting arms…
completely loved.

Oxygen

There will always be treasures
for the noticers.
Magnificent moments
as fleeting as a breeze.
One need only pause
and glance up.
Glowing screens have replaced
the glow of firelight.
The clicking of keyboards
echoes in the absence of conversation.
A text may take moments,
but a prayer is a breath away.

YHWH.
Your Name is a baby's first cry
and death's final whisper.
You are all the oxygen.

Loud

Auditory anarchy.
L O U D!
Chest tightens,
my lungs trapped
in the prison of my ribs.
R A G E!
Uncontrollable.
Helpless.
Nosediving into the spiral.
"Please, turn it down!"
Denied.
Misunderstood;
Miserable.
Too loud, too loud!
I cannot hear myself think,
Nor His still, small voice.

L O S T...
The echoing chamber of
meaningless music and
the cacophony of chaos
pulls me deeper as I
desperately seek
anything to cling to.

Hungry

You've invited me to
sit at Your table,
but I feel more comfortable
gathering crumbs that fall
underneath it.
I cannot accept
my new identity
as Your child.
Shame and guilt
join me as I
navigate my way
across the floor.
I did not anticipate
You meeting me there
with a full plate in Your hands.
You are a God
Who meets us in the mire.

Overcompensation

People who use
ridiculously obscure words
are overcompensating.
They don't want to be
understood.
Just praised.
It's like those prayers
that seem to go on
as if they're monologues.
Louder, more expressive.
More concerned with
being worthy of an Oscar
than heard by the Father.

Sometimes the most fervent prayers
are not intentional.
Moans of pain.
Sighs of exasperation.
Whimpers of hopelessness.

Screaming in my Mazda
at 1am on a Tuesday
is the closest I have been
to the throne of God.

Heavy

Nothing but hate
for a body that's done
nothing but survive.
All the ripping, tearing,
and stretching.
Her soul made manifest
on her flesh.
She lifted heavy,
but it built bitterness
instead of muscle.
Unrecognizable to herself,
squeezing into too-tight denim
and hiding under
hanging hoodies
to obscure her figure.
Nothing but hate
for a body
housing a heart
desperate for love.

Saccharine

Coffee-stained porcelain
piled into a cracked sink.
Tin wind chimes
rattling against a steel door.
A saccharine scent
that halts my steps
and causes me to turn around.

No one can prepare for it,
the small remembrances
that confirm absences.
A gut-twisting, sickly feeling..
the realization that I will never
have another moment
like that with you
this side of eternity.

Tense

It's that uncomfortable moment
when I talk about her
in the past tense.

"She was hilarious."
"What happened to her?"
"She died of cancer at 33."

Pause here.
Options include
over-emphasized shock,
dropping the eyes solemnly,
apologetic sympathy,
or a recollection you have of
someone else you know
who also had cancer.

Don't forget the bit
about God taking the best
for Himself.
Or everything happening
for a reason.
You're right,
and I'll know exactly why
the wrong person
slaps you for that someday.

Condolences

I have always hated
how people immediately
say they're sorry
for your loss.
In high school,
I started saying,
"Me too."
There's also the
uncomfortable pause
that immediately follows.
I scan my mind for
an appropriate segue.
Weather?
Holidays?
News?
I make up
somewhere to be.
Anywhere
but in their pity.

Withdrawals

I attempt to think
of something clever,
but all I have is this pain.
There is nothing cute about it.
No carefully crafted comments
will ease the blow
of life's temporary nature.
I am having withdrawals
from a shortage of joy.
Side effects include
loss of appetite,
increased irritability,
sleeplessness,
and a headache.
Keep calling
on your Physician
for prescription updates.

Red

Using the fire
of your anger
to keep yourself warm.
You'd burn this
whole town down
if you could.
It's like your entire life
is a masquerade ball
and you've forgotten
your true reflection.
Rage is a
comfortable costume
to conceal
a shattered spirit.

Anger is not your transgression,
but how you singe
those closest to you
with its flames.

Caged

Caged birds
don't always sing.
Sometimes they simply
learn to mimic
their surroundings
and grow passive.
Hearts in rib cages
do the same,
unable to imagine
a reality where
they are not broken.
Repetitive phrases
become embedded truths.
My mind is like a parrot,
replaying damaging words
as I commit them to memory.
I don't know if I can fly.
It's not like I've ever
really tried.

Cat Woman

My cat doesn't care
what anyone thinks.
She has excellent boundaries
and no trouble with
expressing her displeasure.
She voices her needs and
clarifies her dislikes
immediately.
Maybe I adore them so much
because I want to be
more like them:
content, curious, and confident.
They even have a special
grace for failure
when they fall.
It's a shame
I never seem to land
on my feet.

Break

When you break a leg,
you can't put your
full weight on it
for a while.
You struggle along
on crutches,
with every task
taking longer than before.

When you break a heart,
you can't put your
full love in it
for a while.
You struggle along
in pieces,
with every emotion
a little stronger than before.

Void

Hemorrhaging hope.
Sensing an endless void.
Descending, bargaining.
Results?
Recurrence.

What about the ones
You don't restore
the way we'd like You to?
A miracle is
good for business.
(Isn't that what
Christianity is these days?)

When You are not
our version of good,
we want a refund.
The mistake is in thinking
You owe us.

You didn't cause the bleeding.
You are the tourniquet.
I'm surprised You haven't
returned us to the void.

Humbled

"I didn't deserve it!
It's not fair!
I've been such
a good person!
I have obeyed God
and served others
with all I have.
Still, He has
allowed me to suffer
violently and
traumatically.
I prayed,
but He did not
change His mind."

If it was
good enough
for Jesus,
I am humbled
to take part.